"Coming Back Stronger Every Time"

Debarupa Bhattacharjee

BookLeaf Publishing

India | USA | UK

Presentation by *BookLeaf Publishing*

Web: www.bookleafpub.com

E-mail: info@bookleafpub.com

ISBN: 9789363315785

First edition 2024

*To all the people who have gone through a lot
in their lives and yet dared to make a
comeback, I dedicate this book to you.*

ACKNOWLEDGEMENT

Creating this poetry collection has been a wonderful journey and I am truly, deeply and eternally grateful to those who have loved me and supported me along the way.

First and foremost, I would like to thank my parents, my father, who is the most important person in my life and who has always been there for me, no matter what, and my late mother, who is always there in my heart and my thoughts and who always encouraged my love for reading and writing.

I would like to thank my friends, family, relatives and acquaintances who have always loved my writing and encouraged me to write more.

I want to thank someone who is just the best listener I have ever had and is also an important part of my life.

To all my English teachers and Professors, my English would have sucked without you. Thank you so much for being such amazing teachers.

To all the writers and poets I met because of my writing account on Instagram, I learn so much from you all every single day, and I am incredibly grateful to have found your writing accounts. You all are fabulous and supremely talented.

I would like to thank all the artists (filmmakers, writers, poets, singers, songwriters, dancers, actors, photographers) whose works have inspired me. As a pop-culture enthusiast, I have learnt the most from these wonderful artists. I am the person I am because they are the artists they are.

To all the neurodivergent people, you all are absolutely brilliant. I have learnt so much from you all in the past few years. Thank you so much for being the wonderful human beings that you are.

To the team at Bookleaf Publishing, thank you for believing in me, giving me this opportunity and helping me in bringing this book to life.

Lastly, I want to thank my readers. Your love for my poetry has given me the encouragement to write and your appreciation means the world to me.

With heartfelt gratitude,
Debarupa Bhattacharjee

PREFACE

'Coming Back Stronger Every Time' is a collection of poems that captures the spirit of strength and resilience of the human soul. It's often during moments of struggle we discover our innate strength and thus find the courage to go on.

The idea for this collection of poems came to me once I had started my poetry account on Instagram. I had started this account when I was going through a particularly challenging period in my life and it had helped me to find hope in times of adversity. It also helped me to gain my confidence back after I had struggled with my mental health for a long time. Some of these poems are personal, some are influenced by my observations about the world we live in, and some are just works of imagination.

I am deeply grateful to the writers and poets I have met because of my writing account and who have consistently supported me with love, encouragement and honest feedback.

This is my first collection of poems, so it will always be special to me. As you read this book, I hope these poems will resonate with you and you will find comfort and a sense of connection in them. May they help you to find hope and peace, just as they did for me.

Warmly,
Debarupa Bhattacharjee

Crimson Coloured Heartache

I look into your hazel eyes
Sparkling like a million fireflies
Making me weak in my knees
As I fall head over heels

You set my life aglow
With a scarlet letter tied to the bow
And a promise that seals
Giving me all the feels

Today, all those promises lie crestfallen
And all those fireflies seem to have changed
direction
And I am left with a crimson-coloured heartache
From your nasty duplicitous blow

From fire and ice
I seek advice
To never lose my heart
And be a fool again

To build myself back

Change my perception

For this crimson-coloured ache

Will keep hurting once in a while

Burn like flames

Reminding me of your treachery and deception

Love Is An Illusion

Love is an illusion

A mystery to many

Elusive, enigmatic, evocative

The more you try to hold it close

The more it slips off your hands

We lose a lot

Trying to find something

That feels like love

That tastes like love

And hugs like love

Yet we don't realise

It's an illusion

Don't get too attached to it

And you'll be set free

If You Knew My Heart

If you knew my heart

You would know how much love it holds

You wouldn't dare to take away its innocence

Drowning it in your seething sea of lies

A part of it forever dies

If you knew my heart

You would not leave it behind

To get caught in a whirlpool of uncertainties

Breathing vapours of sorrow

No hope for a better tomorrow

But, if you knew my heart

You would also know that

I am at my strongest when I am at my weakest

That I can wrap silver ribbons around derelict

dreams and turn them golden

That I can breathe life into stillness

Even when I am broken

Battered Broken Sorrowful Soul

Battered broken sorrowful soul

Drowning dreams unabashed unfold

Wishing the world would ceaselessly see

The bounteous beauty of her precious poems,

untold

Someday she would walk with her head held

high

Hand in hand

With the star-studded sky

Cupid Came With a Knife This Year

Confidence had lost its self-assured home
Demonic wars desecrated the mind's battlefield

Hunched shoulders carried an aching soul
Toxic norms paused soaring dreams

Cupid came with a knife this year
Cut off all ties with a cynical past

Self-love bloomed
Elixir to the soul
One day at a time
Healed and whole

Shrouded in Solitude

Shrouded in solitude

I welcome a new-found gratitude

For this life, for this existence

My sanguine heart's language is forgiveness

I open the door

Leaving behind memories soar

Dancing mildly to the flowery rhythms of my
heart

A song of spring announces a fresh new start

I know the road is long

And probably even filled with thorns

But, I'll find a way to the roses

My confidence speaks

As the Pandora's box of insecurities closes

Solitude has given me more than I had expected

Clear water like head sans getting affected

Shrouded in solitude

I breathe in and out

As the sun shines brightly

Removing clouds of doubt

Lately, I Have Been So in Love With Myself

Lately, I have been so in love with myself that
even on days when my hair is all messy and I
look like I haven't slept in a while,
I can only see beauty and originality and a soul
that shines brighter than the sun

Lately, I have been so in love with myself that I
have cut myself off from anyone who has tried
to disturb my peace, my mental well-being
Tried to make me feel I was not enough

Lately, I have been so in love with myself that I
have forgiven myself for all those mistakes
made in the past
For putting others before me
For putting in them so much trust

Lately, I have been so in love with myself that I
have started taking care of her like I would take
care of someone else
That I have allowed myself to rest whenever I
have felt like
To just disappear and not be stressed

Lately, I have been so in love with myself that I
have accepted myself the way I am
With all my frailties
With all the cracks and holes
With all the quirks and eccentricities
With all the charm and oddities

Because I have realised that I am human
That I can only be the masterpiece that I am
if I am allowed to be the mess

What If We Stopped Caring What the World Thought?

What if we stopped caring what the world
thought?
Would we still do everything that we do?
Or would we do them differently?

What if we stopped caring what the world
thought?
And painted the sky red
And drew beyond the borders
Beyond the limitations placed on our art
And our minds

What if we stopped caring what the world
thought?
And chased a dream that we saw with open eyes
And chased it to the end of the world

What if we stopped caring what the world
thought?

And wrote a book at 50

And painted a masterpiece at 60

And became our best versions at 70

What if we stopped caring what the world
thought?
Would our hearts be full of peace
And minds finally free?

Hope Comes In Many Ways

Andy Dufresne said in The Shawshank
Redemption
"Hope is a good thing
Maybe the best of things
And no good thing ever dies."

And I realised this when I was going through the
lowest phase of my life
That hope comes in ways you don't often notice
Because you are sometimes too busy counting
your curses

But hope is always there waiting for you to pick
it up
In little things, in tiny gestures
In a child's smile
In the moon's soft glow across the sky
How the sun continues to rise after a long dreary
night
How a song inspires you to fight another fight

In the clean water that you drink

In the warm meals that you get to eat

How your body supports you even after

everything it has been through

And how you are blessed enough to dream a

dream

To give it your all

And make it come true

Not Out

Sitting on a weathered bench

Under the gloomy skies

My shoulders hunched

My legs, worn out

From years of carrying the burden

of the world's sighs

Here, I have often wondered if goodness comes

with a price

If what I was told were all lies

Because sometimes the beacon of light has to

endure all the darkness within

Springs of kindness are followed

by winters of longing

And in the end, the question is,

'Is it all worth it?'

I don't know if it is or not

But, I am not ready to give up on goodness just

as yet

Because deep down I know

There is a lot of power in being good

In my honesty, in my pride

In going against the stride

So, right now, I might be low

Bearing the weight of all that sorrow

But, trust me, this, what you see is not going to

be the end of my story

Every tear I have shed will turn into fury

I'll fight the fight

With all my might

In the stillness of the quiet

My strength resides

Of my unyielding strength, I have no doubt

Because even though I am down

I am not yet out

Nature's Healing Touch

17

Autumn's whispered tales

In russet and golden lace

The sky paints a dreamscape of views

A serene escape from my midweek blues

I can feel the amber leaves swaying in the gentle

breeze

This very moment I have always wanted to seize

The golden wheat field takes me in its tender

embrace

In nature's healing touch, my anxious mind finds

solace

A Moonlit Night Never Disappoints

The luminous moon shines in all its glory

Across the deep blue night sky

Stars like little pieces of silver coins

Scattered across the vastness

Rows of buildings appear in silhouettes

And here I am again

Seeking company for my lonely heart

A moonlit night never disappoints

I have walked miles in its gracious embrace

Salving my anxious soul

Away from the gropes of the rapacious reality

Gazing at the milky glow

I sing, I dance, I compose verses

Upon the blank leaves of my inspired mind

And I wonder

How many have come here before

And will continue after me

Concluding their search for poise in eternity

Letting Go

There is a suitcase of unwanted load

In the fold of your memories

Consisting of irrational fears

And unloved territories

Find the strength to bury it

In the cemetery of the past

Let go of the baggage

And mend your heart

You Don't Need a Lot To Be Happy

You don't need a lot to be happy

Clear blue skies

White fluffy clouds

Tangerine sunsets

Rainy nights

A roof over your head

Warm meals on the tour table

Someone to love

Sometimes, it can be yourself

Rest is just an illusion

You can run after

 But you can never have enough

My Spirit, So Strong

My spirit, so strong

Try hammering it

Battering it

I'll come out unscathed

Leaving you in pieces

Liberty is Her Birthright

Her heart feels light today
Like a heavy weight has been lifted off her chest
Age-old societal *diktat* could no longer
keep her under hold
Her starlit dreams float free
She feels like a bird amidst many
Her wings of freedom take flight
She has made this choice
She knows it, it's her destiny
Her nonconformist spirit flies over river-deep
mountains-high
Dancing a dance, the fire in her soul ignites
She paints her mind's canvas with colours she
likes
Liberty is her birthright
It tastes so sweet
Today, she has realised

Don't Let Them Take Your Beauty Away

People bully you emotionally

To make you common

 To make you one of them

Don't let them take your beauty away

What is Beauty?

24

Beauty is everything you've seen

Grace, courage and empathy you've developed

Becoming a part of your soul

Manifesting in your personality

Self-belief is The Cradle Of Love

Self-belief is the cradle of love

In self-belief, love quietly rests

Seeds of self-belief planted early

Leads to the blossoming of self-love unbridled

limitless

Toss out unwanted fears and insecurities

Embrace self-belief and love endless

Life is too precious and too valuable a gift

To crumble in doubt, absolutely clueless

Home

How beautiful it is to build yourself

Step by step

Little by little

After you've been broken and lost

Like a child searching for a home

Not knowing all this while

That it all starts and ends with you

That you were your home all along

Go To Nature

27

If you think it's not going to get better for you

Then let me tell you that,

"I was saved"

By the warmth of the sun

The embrace of the open sky

And the gentleness of the moon

So if you are feeling lost today

Go to nature

And you will find your way back to you

My Soul is Happy

28

My soul is happy.

I feed her love these days.

I Have a Dream

I have a dream

Akin to Lennon's Imagine

To live in a world

Where peace reigns supreme

I have a dream

Where minorities won't have to fight for equality

And everyone would believe in beauty in

diversity

I have a dream

Where self-love is the highest priority

And your worth isn't always measured in terms

of your productivity

I have a dream

Where people will just let you be

No questions, no judgements

No proclamations necessary

I have a dream, to dream big

And dream as much as I want to

Where no one will tell you

You don't have the right to dream free

Vintage Art

She was like vintage art

A bit of wear and tear

Here and there

But, they only made her a kind of beautiful

That forever finds a place

In the depths of your heart

Hope Was Sprawling In

Hope was sprawling in

Where dreams had met a sudden death once

Today, I choose to live

Freedom

32

Taping up broken glass

Sorry doesn't fall off her lips anymore

Her tongue has tasted blood

And her heart knows freedom

Dear Little Me

Dear Little Me,

Happy Birthday!

Can you hear me?

I am talking to you from the other side

Yes, that's me in the mirror

I am your reflection, your future

It's just you and me in this moment

I am here only for a little while

So without wasting even a minute

I want to tell you that,

"You are a great kid

And I am proud of you"

You are going to do

such wonderful things in life

Travel to faraway lands

Across the oceans and seas

Meet the most amazing people

See the most extraordinary things

There is so much to look forward to

On your journey

I want you to remember a few things

No matter what, never let anyone make you feel

less

You are perfect just the way you are

Don't let anyone tell you otherwise

And always be kind

To yourself and others

God knows the world needs more of that

Life is a gift

There are going to be ups and downs

But, towards the end,

You will come out stronger and wiser

Dream big, while chasing your dreams

Always hold on to three things

Hope, hard work and patience

They will take you far

I have to go now

I am glad I could see you

Goodbye Little Me

I love you!

Who Am I?

If you ask me, who am I?
I am going to tell you that
I am not the 'good girl' stereotype
Nor the 'bad girl' prototype
I am just someone
Who had never really known
What was her type

You can't pigeonhole me into any fixed standard
Because on some days, I am as calm as a
meditating monk
On other days, I am as turbulent as a raging
storm

But yes, if there is something that defines me
It's my obsession with my own special interests
Which gives me a sense of normalcy
When I am focusing on my own interests
My mind works faster than a
Jonty Rhodes catch

And in that moment, I feel like I am hard to
match
I have also often felt lonely because of being
different
Because I thought I was a misfit
But, all I needed was the right strategy to
implement

Over the years, I have learnt to use my special
interests the right way
And I have indeed realised
If I give it my all
I can make my own contributions to the world
Only if to people's judgements, I don't fall prey

If they ask for the stars
I aim for the moon
They have tried to rip me apart
But, I know I am still going to bloom

In a world where everyone is supposed to
conform

I am aware that doing your own thing is an act
of rebellion
But, maybe that's who I am
A rebel, a late bloomer, a child at heart
Who wants to make her mark in a billion

You Deserve Love and Care

Unwashed laundry, dirty dishes in the sink
Messy hair, seven tabs open in the brain
You want to move
On certain days, the world feels no less than a
burden
On days like these, read poems about
heartbreaks and moving on
Think of road trips with good people
Or maybe a solo one with the wind in your hair
Be proud of the little things that you've
accomplished
One quote at a time
One day at a time
Order your favourite food
Take a walk in nature
Dance to a tune only you can hear
Believe me when I say you deserve it
Yes, you deserve all that care

Solitude Is My Soul's Holiday

To read for hours

Without anyone's intrusion

To eat your comfort food

Cosy in your PJs

Hair in a messy bun

To watch your favourite movies and romanticise
life

To walk towards the horizon leisurely

To explore quaint little places unhurriedly

To write and get better at it

Slowly and steadily

Solitude has never let me down

It has made me realise

That I could count on myself more than anyone
else

That I could love myself more than anyone else

Solitude has made me a stronger person

A more confident and self-dependent person

It has always given me a safe place to replenish

my soul

And go back and face the world

Solitude is undoubtedly my soul's holiday

Without any pretence

Where I could just let myself be